HAPPY

Birthday

Nana

We love to receive reviews from our customers. If you had the opportunity to provide a review we would greatly appreciate it.

Thank you!

Birthday

I Wrote This Book For You Nana!

Created By:

Birthday Year:

My Age: yrs

1

We celebrate your birthday on..

MONTH ______________________

DAY ________________________

I love birthday cake!!

2

Happy Birthday Nana. I wrote this book for you because.....

3

This is a drawing of us together on your birthday.

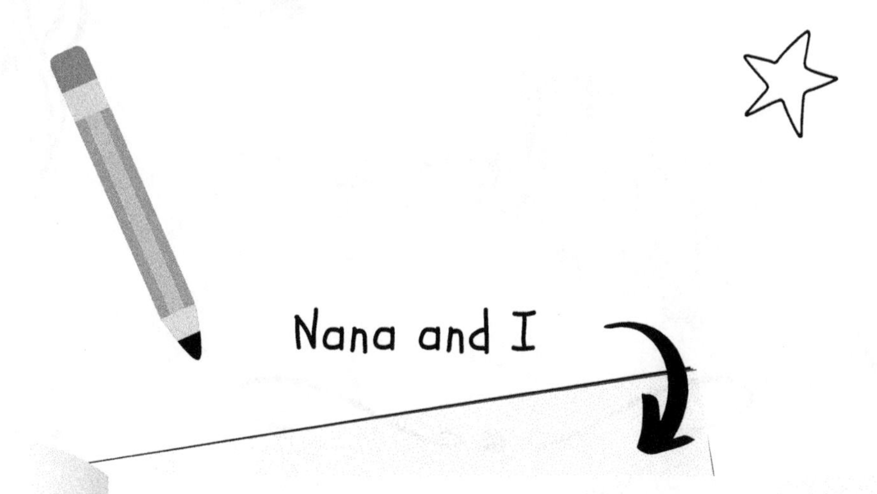

4

I LOVE YOU BECAUSE...

5

Nana, my favorite place to visit with you is....

6

These are 3 things you do that are kind.

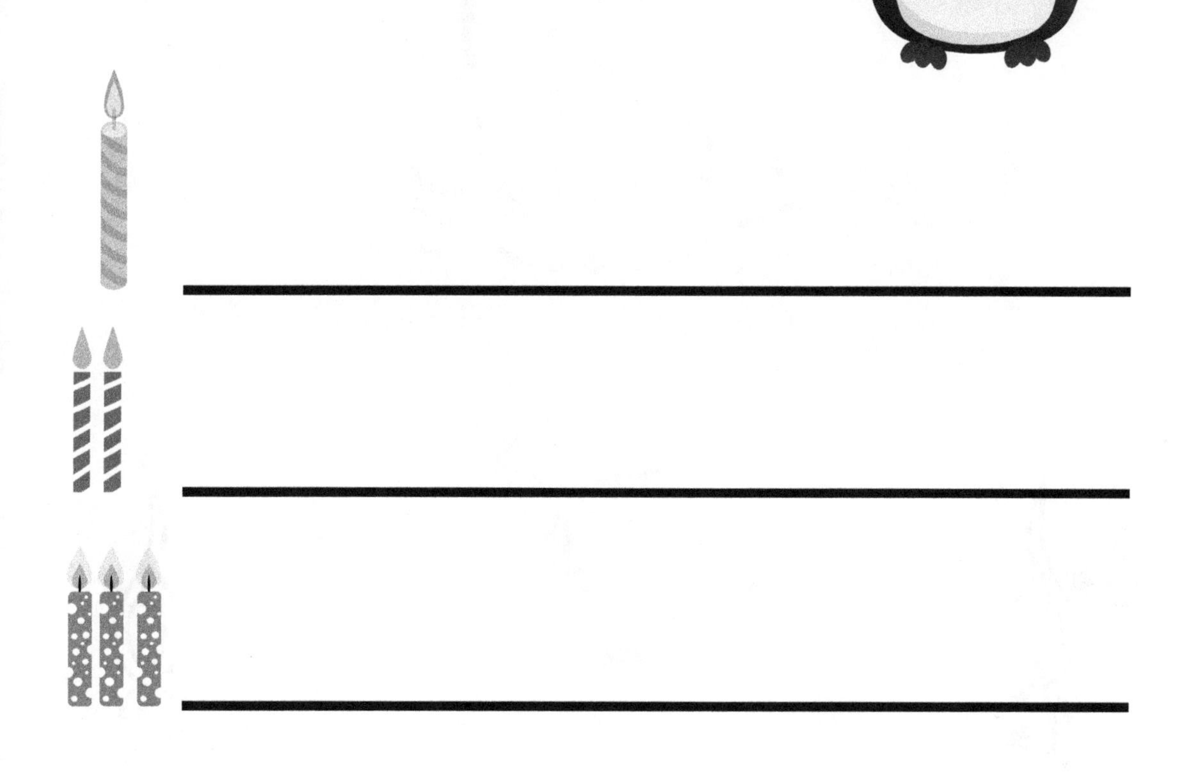

7

My favorite birthday food is...

8

Place your hand here and trace around it with a pencil

9

You like to relax by doing this..

____

____

____

____

10

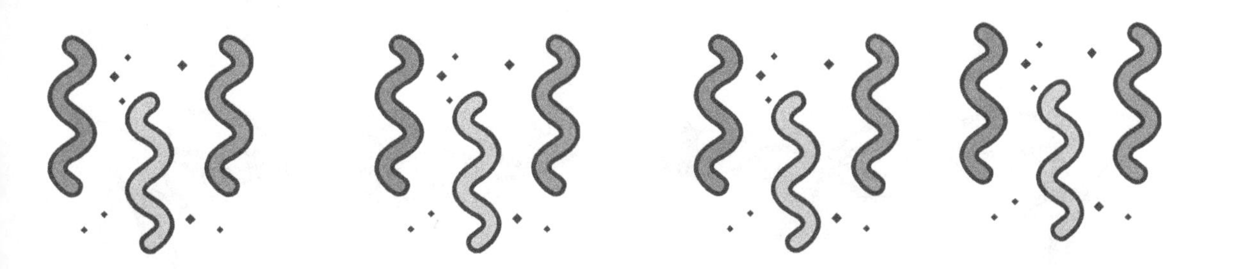

My favorite photo!

11

I would like you to teach me how to do this...

12

If I could get you anything in the whole wide-world for your birthday it would be...

13

You make me laugh when..

14

If I created a birthday t-shirt for you, it would look like this...

15

You can do this better than anyone else!

16

This is a drawing of us on your birthday.

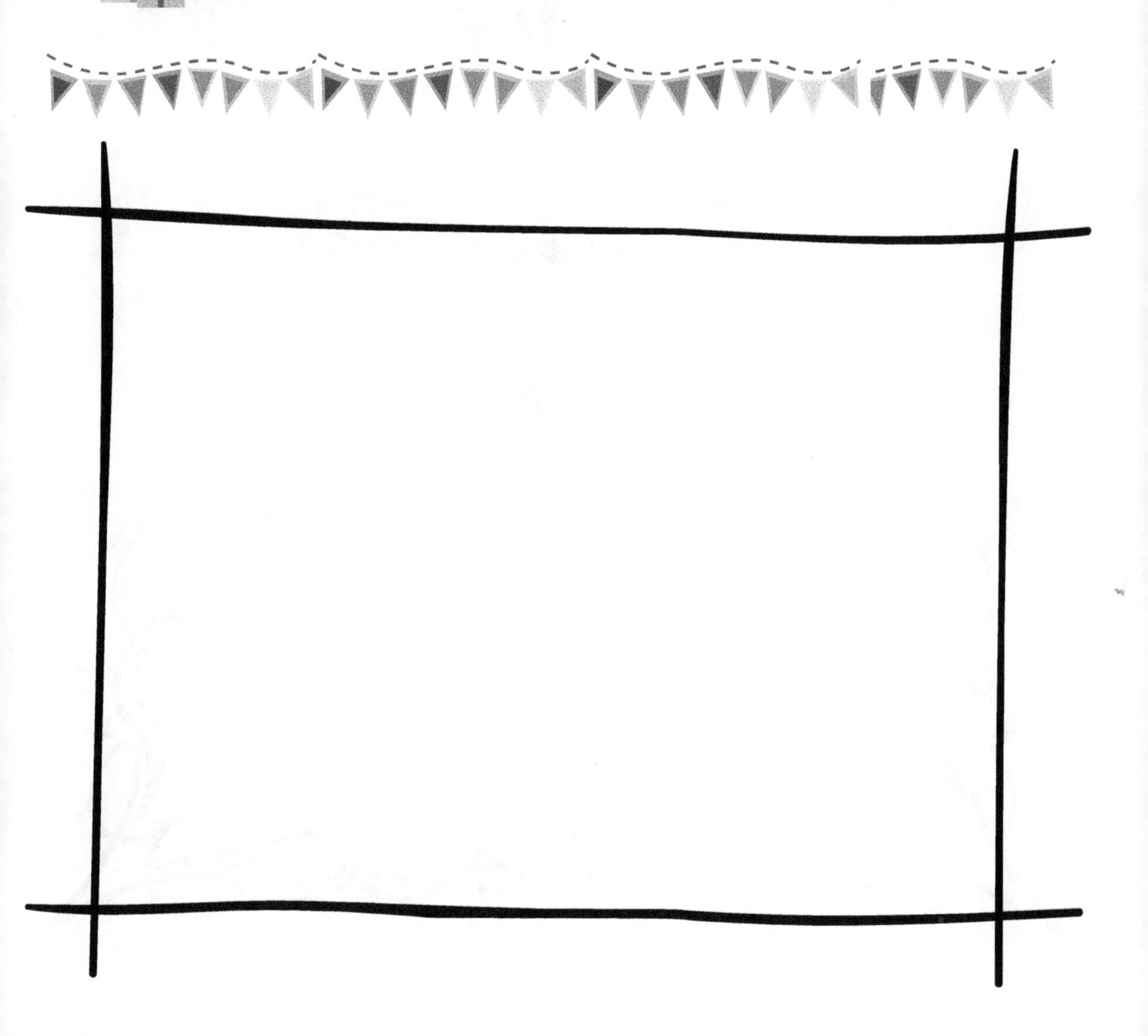

17

I hope that one day we can do this together..

18

You cook the best.....

19

I colored in this birthday cake for you!

20

These are 3 words that best describe you.

1 ______________________________

2 ______________________________

3 ______________________________

SPECIAL MOMENTS or MEMORIES

Add other special photo's or drawings here

SPECIAL MOMENTS or MEMORIES

Add other special photo's or drawings here

SPECIAL MOMENTS or MEMORIES

Add other special photo's or drawings here

SPECIAL MOMENTS or MEMORIES

Add other special photo's or drawings here

Color me in!

THIS HAS BEEN MY SPECIAL BIRTHDAY GIFT THAT I HAVE CREATED FOR YOU.

I HOPE YOU LIKE IT!

A sample of other books created by Romney Nelson

www.thelifegraduate.com/bookstore

CPSIA information can be obtained
at www.ICGtesting.com
Printed in the USA
LVHW022116120121
676186LV00011B/495